LAND THAT JOB!
INTERVIEW INSIDER

Expert Advice on How to Nail
that Job Interview

CONTENTS

Title Page	1
ABOUT THE AUTHOR	5
INTRODUCTION	6
CHAPTER 1: BEFORE THE INTERVIEW	7
Cover Letters	8
A Word About Must-Haves	9
Resumes	11
CHAPTER 2: SOFT SKILLS	12
Placement of Soft Skills	19
CHAPTER 3: OTHER IMPORTANT TOOLS	20
Social Media	21
CHAPTER 4: THE RIGHT LOOK	23
Body Language	25
CHAPTER 5: THE INTERVIEW	30
The Questions	31
CHAPTER 6: POWER WORDS	35
Specific Jargon	37
Additional Interview Tips	39
CHAPTER 7: AFTER THE INTERVIEW	40
AUTHOR'S NOTE	42

ABOUT THE AUTHOR

Becky Gosky lives in the mountains of North Carolina with her husband, two sons, Mom, and two dogs. After spending many years working in human resources and real estate, she now enjoys sharing her expertise as a freelance writer and author. In addition, as a certified coach, she also helps others follow their hearts and passions so they can lead more fulfilled lives whether in a job or their own business. It's a journey she understands on a personal level.

INTRODUCTION

You've done everything you can to land that dream job; attended the best program, maybe obtained additional certificates or training, been to more networking events than you can count, memorized the names and faces of everyone at the company. Ok, maybe the last one is a bit extreme, but the point is, the moment has come to land that job. It's time for the INTERVIEW! If only there was some way to find out what potential employers want—a way to get inside their brains... WAIT, there is! That's what the *Interview Insider* is all about.

The *Interview Insider* is a peek into the minds of employers. In this book, you'll learn about the interview process from an employer's point of view. What does a "dream employee" look like? What qualifications do employers most desire in their employees? What characteristics are they looking for?

Along the way, you'll hear from leading experts. You'll also learn the silent cues interviewees send employers throughout the interview process. As well as the cues interviewers may be sending you. Finally, the *Interview Insider* will examine several pitfalls to avoid and help you unearth new language to help land the job of your dreams.

CHAPTER 1: BEFORE THE INTERVIEW

You wouldn't expect your favorite football team to go straight to the Super Bowl without practice or playing the regular season, nor should you go straight to an interview without some preparation. In fact, it might seem strange to think, but most of your interview hard work and effort actually takes place before you ever say a word to your interviewer.

One of America's first great entrepreneurs, Benjamin Franklin put it this way, "By failing to prepare, you are preparing to fail."

So let's get started!

COVER LETTERS

Cover letters are many people's least favorite part of the job search, an unnecessary evil they're forced to conform to due to some long-lost ancient tradition initiated in a bygone era. While they do take a little extra time and effort, think of them as your one shot. If you don't say something important or impressive, you'll never make it to the coveted interview where you can dazzle potential employers.

It might help to think of your cover letter as your 2-minute story. Nothing is less interesting to an employer than a boring cover letter. You know the type...

Dear Sir or Madame, I am writing in regard to the job posted on... yuck!

If you don't want to read it, why would they? If you were forced at gunpoint to read something like that, would you remember it? Accept for the odd scenario, it's doubtful you'd remember any of the letter.

A cover letter should be interesting, exciting, inspirational, possibly funny, or convey something that sets you apart from everyone else. It's your written ad selling your services.

Think about the opening line of a good book, inspirational song, or your favorite movie. They all did something to make you want to know more. Employers want to read something that makes them want to know more too.

A WORD ABOUT MUST-HAVES

A cover letter should always be addressed to a specific human being. <u>Never ever</u> *To whom it may concern*, or *Dear Sir or Madame*. If you do this, you might as well throw the letter or email in the trash. No one wants to read that. If you don't bother to find out who the employer or person in charge of hiring is, why should they bother to find out who you are?

When you address your cover letter to a human, even if it isn't correct person, you're holding that person accountable to either read it or pass it on to the rightful owner. It also demonstrates to the employer that you can problem solve, research, and self-start. The simple act of putting a name on your cover letter demonstrates that you have skills they need.

While your enclosed resume states your qualifications, don't assume that an employer will read it. Make sure to list a few qualifications in the cover letter. The goal is to make things as easy as possible for a potential employer. If you have something you want them to see or something you're incredibly proud of, either provide the exact link (and double check to make sure it works), or include an attachment or copy of that important project.

Bill Gates once joked he would always hire the laziest person he could find, because they would find the easiest way to get the job done. While he might have been only half kidding, it's not wise to get lazy with most employers before the job even starts. Especially in the initial stages of your contact, your job is to make things as easy as possible for them.

<u>Never ever</u> tell an employer to Google you or your work. The less work for them, the better chance for you.

Finally, after all your hard work crafting the perfect letter, make sure to include your contact information. Always provide a phone number as well as an email and street address. If you have a website, include it as well.

The majority of your cover letter should be devoted to your story. Remember, like the first line of a good book or opening scene of a movie, you want something that will grab and hold a potential employer's interest. This is a great place to demonstrate some of your soft skills, (which will be covered later in this book) such as creativity, persuasion, or collaboration.

Some great ways to open a letter include a mutual contact or friend, a short story that highlights one of your traits or successes the employer might be seeking, or an anecdote or quote that relates to the position, or something that exemplifies your passion for the position or field of work. Most employers are in their jobs because they really like what they do. It makes sense that they'd want to surround themselves with like-minded individuals who share their passion.

Renee West, the President and C.O.O. of the Excalibur Hotel & Casino in Las Vegas put it well when she said, "You can have the best strategy and the best building in the world, but if you don't have the hearts and minds of the people who work with you, none of it comes to life."

Make sure to keep the cover letter brief. To be honest, most employers know by the end of the first paragraph if they're interested in hearing more from you. There's no reason to go on for more than a page. And please don't try the smaller font or decreasing the margins tricks. We know them. We've tried them. Move on.

If you would like up-to-the-minute information in a quick, easy-read format, read our other book in this series, "Land That Job! Write Captivating Cover Letters with No Silly Mistakes," by Becky Gosky.

RESUMES

Like cover letters, resumes need to be neat, clean, and to the point. They are simply a precise, measurable timeline of your accomplishments. Employers don't want to search for information. They want to be able to see all they need to know at a glance.

For those just starting their careers, resumes don't need to be more than a page. Time is valuable, and Interviewers don't want to weed through the lemonade stand you started in the sixth grade or the unpaid internship you had with you had with your uncle freshman year in high school, if you're a trade school or college graduate. I want to see real, relevant work experience from your recent training.

For a while it was a big deal to put a career goal or ambition at the top of a resume. Don't do it. It wastes precious time and space. Employers would much rather see what skills you bring to the table. This is your place to showcase the best of you. The things that don't fit in other places on your resume. This is where you can list several hard skills such as "html expertise" or "crisis mitigation." But it's also a place to list your soft skills such as "creativity" or "reliability."

If you would like more about the secret sauce of a compelling resume, read our other book in this series, "Land That Job! Resume Writing Advice from the Experts," by Becky Gosky.

CHAPTER 2: SOFT SKILLS

A while back, one of the survey questions on Family Feud was to *name something you know is real, even though you can't see it.* Psyched up, the faster button pusher shouted, "bigfoot." To which, Steve Harvey and the audience erupt in laughter.

Like the survey question, soft skills are one of those things employers know exist, even though they can't immediately be seen. Peter Schutz, former President and C.E.O. of Porsche used to say, "Hire character. Train Skill."

So how do interviewees showcase something that isn't easy to convey through traditional methods? And what are the soft skills employers most want?

There are two ways to showcase your soft skills. The smart interviewee will find a way to incorporate both into the selection process.

On Paper. As mentioned above, the first is to include a few soft skills on your resume. You might feel a bit weird about claiming non-concrete attributes. After all, how do you prove them? Isn't labeling your soft skills like bragging? Possibly, but remember this is your chance to sell yourself. If you don't have the confidence to sing your own praises, who will? Besides, employers are more than aware of the importance of these skills. Warren Buffet once mused, "Somebody once said that in looking for people to hire, you look for three qualities: integrity, intelligence, and energy. And if you don't have the first, the other two will kill you."

A word to the wise. While soft skills are easier to fake than hard skills, most employers have plenty of experience spotting fakers. After all they often spend days interviewing candidates for the position you hope to land. So don't fake it and don't add soft skills you haven't mastered.

A good rule of thumb is to use a one to two model. Add one soft skill for every two hard skills on your resume. But be sincere in the soft skills you highlight. Only capitalize on those standout skills or traits you feel are your best.

Bring those soft skills home during the interview process. Prepare anecdotes or have a few situational stories ready to share in which you clearly displayed the soft skills you want to convey to a potential employer. For example, if you want to showcase reliability, relate an event in which your reliability helped save the day or benefitted a former family member, team, or boss.

During the Interview. In some situations, you can demonstrate the soft skills you wish to highlight during the interview process. Good listening skills, creativity, and problem solving are all skills that can be seen and proven in real time.

John Sesay, co-author of *A Lion Has No Horns* builds his book around the tactics he used to save an interview through a combination of soft and hard skills. During the interview, he noticed how distracted his interviewer was. She was so distracted, that he began to wonder if she was taking the interview seriously, or if he was just there to fulfil an EEO requirement.

He noticed that she got most distracted when people dropped reports into the basket on her shelf. She kept reaching up to touch the shelf every time they came by. At first, he thought, she was distracted by the constant flow of workers, but they were quiet and respectful as they soundlessly dropped their work off. The more he watched he realized that the woman's shelf was slightly askew. He finally worked up the courage to ask her if there was a problem with her shelf. She told him that, it had been a problem for over a week and that despite putting in multiple requests for maintenance to fix it, it had yet to be done.

Sesay asked if he might take a closer look at the shelf, which she allowed. Then told her he could fix it, if she could find him a few simple tools. Within minutes, he displayed strong observation, problem solving, and leadership skills, as well as a good dose of empathy. Of course he had the hard skills to carry through and fix the shelf. All of which helped him in the end.

While not everyone will be lucky enough to be presented with a situation like Sesay during an interview, there usually are ample opportunities to showcase soft skills. So, what are the top soft skills employers seek?

According to a 2019 LinkedIn Survey, the top five soft skills employers are looking for are:

1. *Creativity*
2. *Persuasion*
3. *Collaboration*
4. *Adaptability*
5. *Time management*

I would argue an additional five skills:

1. *Reliability*
2. *Energy*
3. *Honesty*
4. *Eagerness to learn*
5. *Empathy*

…also rank high on many employers' must have lists. Let's look at each of them and why they rank among the most important traits employers seek.

Creativity is the foundation on which everything else is built. Whether you're a graphic artist, teacher, or engineer, creativity innovates and problem solves. It brings something new, unique, and different to the table. It helps companies to work smarter not harder. Creative people have great imaginations and aren't afraid to ask "what if?" It's not difficult to see why employers look for creative souls.

Potential employees can showcase their creativity in a number of ways from the design style of their resumes, to providing a link to a website that showcases a project they've helped create, to how they answer interview questions. The possibilities are endless.

Jeff Bezos, founder of Amazon believes creativity and innovation are one and the same. He's quoted as saying, "One of the only ways to get out of a tight box is to invent your way out."

Persuasion is a must for any sales position, but it's also helpful for many other careers. Those with the power of persuasion hold great power. Whether it's fundraising, convincing a board to adopt a new curriculum, or lobbying for new laws, those that can easily and diplomatically sway others to a desired opinion are great assets to any company.

Collaboration or fitting easily into a team is definitely a welcome asset in most industries. Steve Jobs, co-founder of Apple built his business model on collaboration. "My model for business is The Beatles: They were four guys that kept each others' negative tendencies in check; they balanced each other. And the total was greater than the sum of the parts."

While collaboration might seem obvious, the reality is many organizations face personality conflicts. Big egos, the need for power, competition, past histories and more can lead to fractures within organizations. Sometimes these situations brew for years, creating toxic work environments.

Those who are willing to work together, rift off each other, credit the team for good work, and so on make for a more desirable work environment and therefore are more desirable employees. Some qualities collaborators exhibit include: conflict management, strong listening skills, giving positive feedback, and the ability to mediate and negotiate.

Adaptability fits well with the old adage the "best-laid plans…" It's an old Scottish saying that basically means planning for something doesn't guarantee its success. That couldn't be truer in the workplace. Whether it's a key piece of equipment that breaks at the worst moment, an employee who doesn't show up, or a shipment that doesn't arrive, there will always be reasons for flexibility and back-up plans. Those who can go with the flow or hop into a different position without complaint when needed most rank high on employers must have lists. Those who are adaptable remain calm in a crisis, are able to analyze a situation and quickly self-manage or perhaps even organize a small group to problem solve or cover a needed task.

Time Management is akin to money. Those who can work smarter not harder usually accomplish tasks in less time, which saves money. In the book *The 4-Hour Work Week*, author Timothy Ferriss introduces the concept that time is just as valuable as money. The more of it that we can save, the more we can devote to the tasks we really want to be doing. Likewise, the more a company can save, the more it can devote to doing what it was intended to do as opposed to the mechanics or housekeeping of the business. Time managers are self-starters, that not only know how to plan, but also delegate.

Reliability doesn't take much to accomplish. After all it's about showing up, being dependable, and following through. Yet it's a critical soft skill for potential hires. Could you imagine what would happen if you planned a transcontinental trip and the pilot didn't show up? You don't necessarily have any desire to become friends with the pilot or even know her name, but you absolutely need her to show up for her job. And you expect that when she arrives, she not only knows how to properly fly the plan, but can do it well enough to get you safely to your destination.

In the same way, an employer may not want to be your best friend, but they count on those they hire to do a specific job well and in the allotted amount of time. If you want to display reliability during the interview process first and foremost arrive on time. Then make sure to share a past experience in which your reliability was key.

Energy is often equated with positivity. Those who have tins of energy can sweep in and brighten the disposition of an entire organization. Someone with energy is motivated to go the extra mile, work quickly and competently. Likewise, those who lack energy are often seen as weights pulling everyone down with them. They distract others from their work or cause others to pick up their slack. It's not difficult to see why employers enjoy hiring those with lots of energy. They just seem to make life easier.

Honesty is a soft skill that was somewhat overlooked in the past, but is enjoying a resurgence in the professional world. Sometimes also referred to as ethics, social responsibility, or integrity, this soft skill has made a huge comeback especially in environmental, eco-friendly, grassroots type businesses. But it has also made it to the corporate world—where cutting corners to save a dime is seen as less and less desirable.

Honesty isn't just about doing what looks right to the outside world, it's about expressing values on which an organization was founded. Most organizations today have a mission statement or history on their websites. Find out what's important to the founding members. If their values fit with yours, use similar language during your interview to convey your honesty.

Eagerness to Learn might seem a bit counterintuitive but nothing could be further from the truth. Most employers understand there will be a learning curve when a new employee joins their organization. Think of it like learning to drive a car. They expect you to know how to drive, but understand that you may only know how to drive an automatic while they operate a manual. Or better yet, maybe you know how to drive both, but it's still wise to have a look around the new car and learn where everything is before putting it into gear and taking off. It's great to display your knowledge and know-how, but it equally important to listen and learn. Those who do come to understand not only what is expected of them, but what the organization wants to do, where it hopes to go, and how those within it relate to each other.

Empathy is the ability to understand another person's situation and relate to it. In business it's the exact opposite of "don't let the door hit you on the way out." Businesses and organizations that care about their customers and employees generally last longer and don't have to work quite as hard. Think about it, empathy inspires loyalty. When an organization is empathetic, it retains those who continue to fund it, which is much easier than constantly finding new clients and customers. Those who are empathic consider the needs of others and generally display interpersonal communication skills.

Smile. Some simple ways to display empathy include smiling, calling people by name, remembering them or learning something about them before hand to mention during an interview and taking time to listen.

Arte Nathan, who was the Chief Human Resources Officer for several Vegas Casinos, used to say, "You can't teach employees to smile. They have to smile before you hire them."

Make A Wish. One of the most powerful tools of empathy is the wish. A wish is a way to give someone something without necessarily really doing it. It needs to be sincere, but an example would be if an angry customer came in demanding something be fixed. An empathic employee might start by smiling, and calling the customer by name. Then listening without interrupting. They might then ask the customer what they would like to be done about the situation. Even if it something that the employee can't fix, they could say something like, "I can see how upsetting this is to you. I wish I could fix it for you right now. Let me see if I can find someone who can better help you." Often just the ability to listen, display empathy, and give the customer what they need in the form of a wish, goes a long way to fixing a problem and retaining that customer of the future. In an interview situation, you might share an empathetic experience or suggest a way the organization could display more empathy.

PLACEMENT OF SOFT SKILLS

Now that you understand soft skills and hopefully have identified a few of your own it's time to put them on your resume. Place the "Skills" section directly below your name and contact information in three columns across the top. Then list 9 to 12 bulleted skills that highlight your abilities. That gives employers a better idea of who you are and what you can do for their organization than any goal statement.

CHAPTER 3: OTHER IMPORTANT TOOLS

REFERENCES

It has become commonplace to leave references off resumes with a statement at the bottom such as "references available upon request." Some clever job seekers think this is a great way to shorten their resumes. Remember earlier when we said always make things as easy as possible for an employer? Providing references makes things easier on employers. If you're making things difficult for them before you're even hired, chances are they won't be particularly interested in hiring you. Especially if they are 10 more resumes on the employers desk with references.

If you've tried your best and can't fit references on your one-page resume, you may include a separate references page. Just make sure that your contact information is listed on it as well, in the event that it gets separated from the rest of your information.

SOCIAL MEDIA

Different careers require different must-haves. In this day and age of cyber connectivity, it's very likely a good idea to have a small website. Even if it just has your picture, resume, and a link or two to something career related that you're proud of, having a website shows you're willing to go the extra mile and do something to get noticed.

More importantly, if potential employers like what they see, they very likely will do an internet search of you either before or after an interview. Of course the best thing to do is never to put anything on social media that you don't want a potential employer to see. More than one politician's career has ended over old pictures and posts. But even if you never plan to run for office, or have any idea what the two main political parties in American government are called, be careful what you post. You never know when an interested employer might be turned off by shots of potential employees at a raging kegger or other inappropriate photos.

Make sure your social media pages are well protected from outside eyes and then double check those security features. Many social media sites are not as secure as you might assume. A prime example of this is Facebook. While users can choose their friends and take security measures for who can friend them and see their pages, people can still follow users without their permission. In addition, those who have the app on their phones, can be tracked as they travel to and from home, work, shop and dine. Facebook is not the only example of this. Plenty of social media sites have similar loopholes. These loopholes just may be the thing employers come across when conducting a background check on potential employees.

Once hired, be mindful of posts as well. It's not uncommon to hear stories about employees who call in sick and then post pictures of themselves hanging out at the beach. Or maybe work has been tense, and insulting posts about a boss or another employee surface. Maybe, it happened at a past job. The bottom line? Nothing on the Internet goes away forever and eventually everyone gets access to it. Don't post anything you don't want the world to know. Employers are people too and they use the Internet.

CHAPTER 4: THE RIGHT LOOK

APPROPRIATE DRESS

Just as you wouldn't wear a bathing suit to a cocktail party, the clothes you wear to an interview are important. Yes, we've heard it all before. You're an individual, a nonconformist. People shouldn't be judged by their clothes, but their talent. And on and on it goes. The reality is, right or wrong people are judged by what they wear.

It wouldn't make sense for a fashion designer to hire a person who came to an interview in muddy jeans and a ketchup stained t-shirt. Just like a farmer would raise his brows if a hired hand arrived in a three-piece suit to bail hay. No matter how much the potential employee claims to know or how wonderful their portfolio is, their outer appearance would undermine their interview performance and skill set.

Clothes tell an employer you understand what is expected of you. They also tell him or her a lot about who you are. This has nothing to do with labels or how expensive the clothing is. It has everything to do with social cues, appropriateness and the ability to fit in and be a team player. Your uniform whether it's an actual uniform or the unspoken uniform of the office, tells those you work with that you belong to their group, and sets the tone that you are ready and willing to work.

Many offices have adapted a relaxed dress code, but unless you know that for a fact before an interview, don't show up in cut offs and your favorite university sweatshirt. You don't have to wear a suit and tie or dress (unless the office requires it). But dress pants or khakis, button down shirts or polos, clean shoes (something beside athletic shoes) demonstrate that you are a professional, who at the very least cleans up nicely for this one day. It shows respect for the importance of the job, your employer, and the position. It says, you will take your work seriously and can be an asset to the organization.

BODY LANGUAGE

Whole books have been written on business body language. In fact, it's so important that body language experts are often hired in high profile court cases to help select a jury and read their language during a trial. While beyond the scope of this book, here are a few key points.

Arrival

Make sure you appear confident from the minute you walk in to a professional interview. Some employers like to watch potential employees from a hidden location before they introduce themselves. Use good posture, hold your head up, and speak with confidence even when speaking to the receptionist.

Very often the person at the front desk will take your name and ask you to have a seat. Graciously thank him and move off a few steps but remain standing. Remaining standing tells those around you that you are a busy individual who values time and shouldn't be kept waiting. It also conveys confidence. While it often makes the receptionist nervous, it also makes you difficult to ignore. If you are left waiting too long, they will likely call back to the interviewer to hurry them along, without you saying a word.

While you are waiting, prepare for the interview. If it is winter, take off your coat. Either find a place to hang it, or neatly fold it, and drape it over your left arm. That way you won't have to fumble with it when it is time to shake hands with your right hand and go into your interview.

If you must carry an accessory such as a back pack, brief case, portfolio, or purse, carry only one extra thing. The more things you have, the more difficult it is to maneuver through tight halls and cramped office spaces. You want to appear organized and ready to work or display your skills—not fumble with additional baggage. Women who carry purses might opt instead to carry a portfolio, keep their purse in the car under the seat, and put their keys in a pocket. Anything to downsize and lessen the clutter.

Carrying only one additional item also helps when it comes to that handshake. Items won't have to shifted or set down to make contact.

Handshakes

A firm, not too tight handshake is always best. And interviewee should approach the handshake as equals. In other words, extend your hand from the side to meet an interviewer's hand, as opposed to from above or below. Shaking a hand with your hand on top, sends an inappropriate message of dominance. Whereas shaking you hand from below would silently send a message of meagerness. Likewise grasping their hand in both of yours, sends the inappropriate message of intimacy or being a little too friendly.

Seating

When sitting, men in particular, need to be mindful of spreading out too far. This can be seen on buses or the subway when men sit with their legs spread far apart, arms extended full length across the back of the seats, possibly taking up additional space for coats or packages. On mass transit, it sends the message to stay away (which might be a plus in certain situations). In the office a variation of wide spread legs while seated can be interpreted as overly comfortable, cocky, sloppy, or an inappropriate attempt to exert dominance.

It is best for either gender to sit up straight. Legs should either be flat on the floor, one foot tucked slightly behind the other, or crossed. Hands should be comfortable. Folding them in your lap or keeping them loosely at your sides is always acceptable. If you're an animated speaker, don't be afraid to use your hands, but it might be a good idea to reel it in and keep gestures to a minimum or more conservative than usual.

When in doubt at an interview, err on the side of conservativism. This has nothing to do with politics. With dress, gestures, opinions it's easier to expand on them later than to try to retract them after the fact.

In most U.S. business settings, it's considered good manners to look directly into the eyes of your interviewer. However, in some other cultures this is seen as a challenge or sign of disrespect. Therefore, it's important if interviewing for a job in another country to research local culture and customs ahead of time.

If offered a choice, choose a chair directly across from your interviewer. It's the best way to keep eye contact. It also puts the interviewee and interviewer on equal footing. Standing over someone or sitting in a higher chair or at a higher angle exerts dominance. Sitting to the side, forces others to turn to look at us. Neither of these scenarios is preferable in an interview situation.

If you sit on the far side of a desk from your interviewer, ask before placing your hands or your things on their desk. Doing so without asking can be seen as arrogant, overly confident, assumptive, or pushy.

Attention

Interviewees demonstrate attentiveness by sitting forward in their seat or leaning slightly forward so that their body angles toward the interviewer. An interviewee might also tilt their head toward the interviewer. Of course smiling often conveys interest, as does nodding.

If an interviewer begins to fidget, look away, check their phone, or seems distracted, chances are they've lost interest in what the interviewee is saying. It's a nonverbal cue to move on.

An interviewer that places a hand on their chin or props their head in hand or over their mouth, is likely to be less interested in what an interviewee is saying. Propping a hand on the face is usually a way of trying to stay focused when one has lost interest. Putting a hand over one's mouth could be a way to stifle yawns. However, it could also be a way to subconsciously stop from saying something they would rather not say. This could be as simple as suppressing an opinion or as serious as covering a lie.

Mirroring

Mirroring is the ability to reflect another person's body language in your own. For example, if a person clasps their hands behind their back while speaking to you, you might mirror their body language by doing something similar. A prime example of mirrored body language can be seen by watching Vice President Pence when he's with President Trump. Quite frequently, you might see the President take a drink of water, only to be mirrored a few seconds later by the Vice President.

Mirroring is often done subconsciously. It can be used to express unity or connectivity. But it can also be used to reflect a comfortable or subservient position. If you're not sure what to do or how to act during the interview process, adopt a similar stance to your interviewer.

The Whole Sentence

Reading body language is intuitive, but it's also unique to ever situation. The main thing to remember is that movements and gestures shouldn't be read in isolation. It's important to take in the context of the setting, extenuating circumstances, and the rest of the body sentence.

For example, if an interviewer shivers it might mean that she dislikes what an interviewee says, but she might also be cold. If the interviewer also has a pink nose and rubs her arms, body sentence tells the interviewee she's cold. But if she shakes her head, raises her brows, or looks away, she's likely conveying a less favorable opinion.

As an interviewee, be ready to read the whole-body sentence of your interviewer to help determine what you say and how you say it.

CHAPTER 5: THE INTERVIEW

At last the moment to shine at your interview arrives. The most important thing to keep in mind is to treat it like a conversation. In 1997 Steve Jobs interviewed James Green for a job at Pixar. When Green reflected back on that interview years later he noted that Jobs had him over to his home and "felt we had more of a conversation, than an interview."

A conversation is relaxed and friendly. It involves maintaining good eye contact, active listening, asking relevant questions based on information learned during the conversation, and answering the questions asked—not a running dialogue of your choosing.

THE QUESTIONS

There are several standard questions most interviewers like to ask. While you can't be prepared for everything, there's nothing wrong about thinking and rehearsing the answers to some of these questions ahead of time.

Tell me about yourself?

This question is often used to gauge a little bit about your personality. When interviewers ask this question, they do not want your life story. They're usually looking for a brief answer with a hint of personality. This is the perfect time to mention a unique hobby you have, exotic trip you've taken, or some other piece of trivia about yourself. If you can relate it back to something to do with the job, all the better. But don't try too hard. If it's a stretch or just doesn't make logical sense, don't force the connection.

Tell me about a time when...?

Interviewers love to pull out questions that help them understand how you handle various situations. Some popular variations of this question include *when you displayed leadership skills, had to problem solve, or head a project.* Interviewers are less interested in the situation that lead up to action, than your response. Be honest and have a few situations at the ready should they ask.

Tell me a about a time you made a mistake and how you resolved the issue, what areas do you need to improve in?

These types of questions are also popular. While no one likes to talk about the areas they might come up short, don't dodge the question. The worst answer you can give an employer is to tell them you don't make mistakes or have any shortcomings. All humans fail and can stand to improve in something. Insisting you're perfect or have no issues is dishonest. It also implies you're not open to change or growth. Or worse yet, you may not be willing to take direction. Interviewers seldom want employees who don't listen or are unwilling to take direction.

While you want to give an honest assessment of your capabilities, you don't have to sell yourself short either. There's no need to share the worst thing that ever happened to you at a job or talk about an incident that may have gotten you fired. Pick something truthful, but not necessarily detrimental. Even better, if you can include a key lesson or something of importance that was learned from the mistake or shortcoming, all the better.

Bill Gates notes, "It's fine to celebrate success, but it's more important to heed the lessons of failure."

Doing so displays honesty, an aptitude for growth, flexibility, and possibly an empathy for others that might experience similar situations.

Where do you see yourself in 5 or 10 years?

Elon Musk is known for asking this question along with one other. There are many right answers to this question and one absolutely wrong answer. Unless you are interviewing to be groomed to take over the interviewer's position, never ever tell the interviewer you hope to have their job in a few years. Most interviewers don't want to hire someone who will make them watch their backs at all times. It's also rather presumptuous if not insulting to tell someone that you could do their job just as well as they could, without on the job training or earning your time.

How would you change this company or *what have you seen that you think could be improved here?*

While many interviewers applaud innovative ideas, they also appreciate tact. It's all right to share your ideas. It's not all right to trash the organization in the process. A good critic doesn't criticize everything. Instead he or she reflects in an issue and supplies a positive solution. One of the best ways to tactfully deliver a critique is to sandwich it between positive statements.

One: Start by focusing on some strengths of the organization. "I really like the way X Corp makes each customer feel like an individual by calling them by their names."

Two: Talk about the shortcoming. If you can describe it as something that needs improvement all the better. "I think X Corp could really improve on the way it collects money from customers."

Three: Provide your solution and explain how it might improve the situation. "I think X Corp might see improved sales if you were to offer an online pay option. I think clients might like the convenience of paying on the spot instead of mailing their bills or stopping by to pay."

Four: Conclude with another positive statement as well as the likely positive outcome. "It's great the way X Corp treats everyone like family. No doubt that's why you have so many repeat customers. Adding the online option will not only keep them coming back, but help X Corp bring in more invoices on time."

Suggesting improvements or changes using positive sandwiches is a diplomatic, non-threatening way to convey new ideas, without seeming presumptive, coming off like a know it all, or a corporate climber gunning for the interviewer's job.

Why do you feel you would be a good fit for this job, or why do you want to work for us?

This seems pretty straightforward. While it's all right to tell an interviewer that this is your dream job or something you've hoped to do all your life, interviewers want to hear something bigger than you. They want to hear why your skills are perfect for their organization. Make sure your answer reflects more about how you will be an asset and benefit to them, than how they will help you. Use fewer "I" statements and more "you" statements.

Do you have any questions for me/us?

This is the other question Elon Musk likes to ask. Shaking your head or answering that you think an interviewer has covered everything may seem like the polite or complimentary thing to do, but please this is the time to ask any follow-up questions. If an interviewer asks this question, he or she really wants to know if there is anything else they can share. Asking a question or questions shows that you were actively listening, interested in what they have to say, aren't afraid to speak up, inquisitive, and curious. All of those are great qualities, especially for a growing organization. It is best to have at least one question at the ready to display your soft skills as well as to convey interest and a willingness to engage or collaborate.

Is there anything else you would like to add?

Becky Gosky

This is your last chance to impress, your closing sales pitch. Always add something else. Restate what benefits you would bring to their organization. It could be something you feel is important that the interviewer didn't ask, something you feel he or she misunderstood that needs clarification, or a quick summary of you and your work experiences. Don't be afraid to ask for the job if it feels right.

CHAPTER 6: POWER WORDS

Most people are aware that words have meaning and therefore power. In the interview setting there are two classes of words that tremendously benefit interviewees.

Strong Words

Strong words often come down to verbs that stand alone. When we use them, there's no question what we think or feel. Their meanings are crystal clear. They aren't kinda or sorta. You don't kinda know the president of the university, you know the president of the university. You don't sorta speak French, you speak French.

Strong words don't need helper verbs such as the "be" family (is, are, was, were, be, am, been, should, could, would, has, have, had, might, must, many etc).

Instead of *I have worked* use *I worked.* Better yet change *work* to something that evokes a stronger mental image such as *I created* or *I engineered.*

Strong verbs are concrete action verbs that create mental pictures. They dazzle and pop bringing thoughts, experiences, and qualifications to life.

Instead of "say" use "speak" instead of "make" use "create" or "foster."

Strong words don't hedge or provide disclaimers, they make a statement. Instead of *I think I would be perfect for this job because...* try *I'm perfect for this job because...*

Strong words and writing don't require extra adverbs and adjectives. Stripping extra words away for cleaner text (cover letters and resumes) conveys a position of strength and knowledge.

SPECIFIC JARGON

If you want to be considered for a specific job, you need to speak that organization's language.

Every industry has its own lingo—but many organizations take it a step further with specialized catch phrases or specific company branding.

For example NPR or National Public Radio, no longer references "donations" during fund drives. Instead employees are instructed to use the term "gifts" as in "your gift of $10 a month will help…" the rebranding idea is that people are more likely to give more if they feel they are giving a "gift" rather than making a "donation." Gifts seem like more fun. They make people feel good about themselves, whereas donations are more of an obligation. Someone applying to work in the grant or fundraising department at NPR would seem a lot more knowledgeable and therefore a good hire, if they referenced "gift giving" as opposed to "donations" during their interview.

Another example of this branding comes from the various weather reporting agencies. Once upon a time the Weather Channel created the term "wind chill," which many us take for granted as an actual thing. As it turns out, it's just a term someone there made up to describe what it feels like outside despite the reading on the thermometer. So when Accuweather came along a few years later, it had to come up with a new term to describe this phenomenon that we are all used to hearing about. But it couldn't use the Weather Channel's phrase, so it rebranded its own term and created the aptly named "feels like temperature." Someone hoping to land a job with Accuweather would need to know about the feels like temperature.

A little research on your desired company's website or leafing through a company publication will turn up plenty of gems. Phrases that are used repeatedly as opposed to more traditional language are likely to be the jargon of choice for that company.

Interviewees hoping to get a foot in the door should mirror some of that language not only in their cover letters and resumes, but during the interview process.

ADDITIONAL INTERVIEW TIPS

Show Don't Tell

If you have something truly spectacular to show an interviewer don't just tell them about it. If it's within reason, such as a brochure or blueprints you've designed bring them with you.

Elon Musk of Tesla explains it well. "Everything works in PowerPoint; but if you have the physical item or some demonstration software, that's much more convincing to people than a PowerPoint presentation or a business plan."

Express Yourself

If you have a strong opinion or don't agree with something the interviewer says, find a respectful way to let them know. Sydney Finkelstein, author of *Superbosses: How Exceptional Leaders Master the Flow of Talent,* writes "CEOs are intrigued by candidates who aren't afraid to push back. Have a point of view and be unafraid to disagree with what you're hearing. Superbosses respect, admire, and value people who can do that. They're looking for people who can change the world."

CHAPTER 7: AFTER THE INTERVIEW

At the end of the interview, always verify a time and date that you can expect to hear from the organization and whether to expect a call, text, email or other form of communication.

Thank You

Go home and write an a short but thoughtful thank you email or letter. Take a few minutes to express your gratitude for the opportunity. If there was something that you especially enjoyed or left a lasting impression on you, let the interviewer know.

Writing a thank you note keeps you fresh in the interviewer's mind as he or she considers hires. It also demonstrates more of your soft skills from the ability to follow-up, to interpersonal and communication skills.

Contact

If you don't hear back by the appropriate time, contact the organization. Maybe they lost your contact information or sent an email to the wrong address. Either way you have the right to know and they have an obligation to be accountable.

Getting the Job

If you get the job, congratulations. Confetti for you. Life is good. You can stop reading!

If on the other hand, you're offered the job, but it just doesn't feel right, don't take it. If you come to this conclusion before you hear back from the potential employer, reach out to them and let them know, you've decided to go another way. Potential employers appreciate honesty. By letting them know, you may be saving them time and energy. In the end, you are the one that must live with the decision. If you take a job that you know you're going to miserable at, and quit or be fired in a few months, you're wasting everyone's time. It's not fair to employers who don't want to train someone only to have them leave. And it's not fair to you, who will be stuck doing something you hate instead of chasing that dream job you really want.

Something Better Out There

But what if you get door number three? What if you don't get the job? Know that it's not the end of the world. If you have the opportunity ask what made them go with another candidate, or what you could have done differently. There's never shame in asking questions for self-improvement.

You may want to take a few minutes or perhaps the evening to collect yourself. When you're ready, reflect on the interview experience and what you learned from it. Consider what you could have done better and improve for next time.

If in your heart of hearts you feel there truly is nothing you could have done better, don't waste sleep over it. Always remember interviewers and employers are people too. Sometimes it comes down to personality or the kind of day they had before they made their decision. As Howard Schultz, former CEO of Starbucks says, "Hiring people is an art, not a science."

Elon Musk uses a very personal criteria in making his hiring decisions. "If you have a choice between a lower valuation with someone you really like, or higher valuation with someone you have a question mark about, take the lower valuation."

Just remember, life is all about how you choose to look at things. Look at the choice not to hire you as an opportunity to find something even better. Your perfect job is still out there somewhere, just waiting for you to find it.

AUTHOR'S NOTE

If you liked, "*Land That Job! Interview Insider: Expert Advice on How to Nail that Job Interview,*" please consider reading my other books in the *Land That Job!* Series on Amazon.

Please leave me a review while you are there. Your comments truly shape the future of my work. Thank you!

For more hands-on help, I offer certified coaching through the Your GPS for Life Community. Check us out at www.yourgpsforlife, on Facebook: @yourgpsforlife, and on LinkedIn: linkedin.com/company/yourgps.

You will receive a complimentary thank you gift for contacting us and subscribing!

www.ingramcontent.com/pod-product-compliance
Lightning Source LLC
Chambersburg PA
CBHW070842220526
45466CB00002B/861